ILLUSTRATED GARDENING JOURNAL

D0104361

THE LOVE OF GARDENING IS A SEED ONCE SOWN THAT NEVER DIES.

A garden is an ever changing story;
a narrative that gradually evolves, setting
us back into the slow circles of nature.
As a rule, the more you put in, the more you
get out, but one of the joys of a garden is its
unpredictability. Some plants thrive, others
don't, some harvests have huge yields,
others less so. It can be a very rewarding,
but at times frustrating investment.
In the words of Alfred Austin; "There is
no gardening without humility. Nature is
constantly sending even its oldest scholars
to the bottom of the class for some
egregious blunder."

Keeping a journal will help your gardening
skills develop. By documenting when,
where and how you planted each crop,
you can keep a record of what worked
and what didn't. At the end of the year,
look back through your notes, sift through
the successes and disappointments of
the past months, and start to plan ahead.
Remember, a garden is a sort of laboratory.
The joy is in experimentation. And in the
elusive promise of next year's garden.

DESIGNING
YOUR GARDEN

Use this grid to design your garden. Keep in mind the size of the plants at maturity – it's easy to forget how large those seedlings can grow.

A FEW GARDEN DESIGN TIPS

Make sure to check your soil type either with a PH kit or by hand, and plant accordingly.

Plant bulbs in clumps of 5, 7 or 9.

Create shapes that mirror the rhythm of windows or doors on the house's façade.

Plant warm colours in the shade and cool colours in the light to make the most of their qualities.

Plan a path for easy access to garden essentials (like bins/shed/washing line).

TOOLS

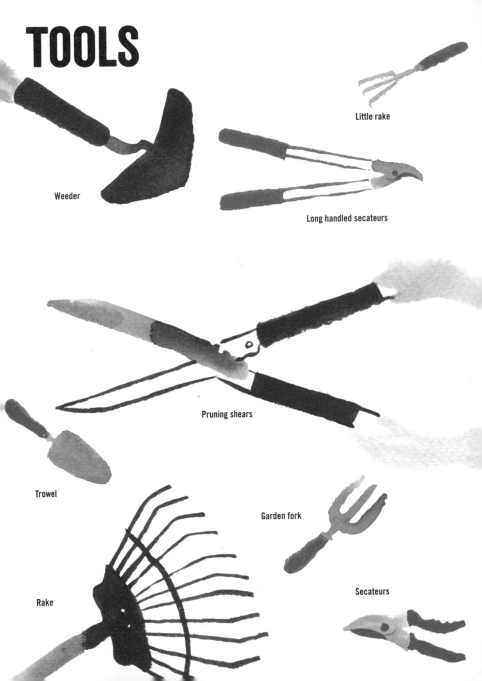

Little rake

Weeder

Long handled secateurs

Pruning shears

Trowel

Garden fork

Rake

Secateurs

SEED STARTING LOG

NAME OF SEED

DATE SOWN

NOTES

DATE SPROUTED

DATE TRANSPLANTED

LOCATION AND LIGHT

NAME OF SEED

DATE SOWN

NOTES

DATE SPROUTED

DATE TRANSPLANTED

LOCATION AND LIGHT

NAME OF SEED

DATE SOWN

DATE SPROUTED

DATE TRANSPLANTED

LOCATION AND LIGHT

NOTES

NAME OF SEED

DATE SOWN

DATE SPROUTED

DATE TRANSPLANTED

LOCATION AND LIGHT

NOTES

NAME OF SEED

DATE SOWN

NOTES

DATE SPROUTED

DATE TRANSPLANTED

LOCATION AND LIGHT

NAME OF SEED

DATE SOWN

NOTES

DATE SPROUTED

DATE TRANSPLANTED

LOCATION AND LIGHT

NAME OF SEED

DATE SOWN

DATE SPROUTED

DATE TRANSPLANTED

LOCATION AND LIGHT

NOTES

NAME OF SEED

DATE SOWN

DATE SPROUTED

DATE TRANSPLANTED

LOCATION AND LIGHT

NOTES

NAME OF SEED

DATE SOWN

NOTES

DATE SPROUTED

DATE TRANSPLANTED

LOCATION AND LIGHT

NAME OF SEED

DATE SOWN

NOTES

DATE SPROUTED

DATE TRANSPLANTED

LOCATION AND LIGHT

NAME OF SEED

DATE SOWN

NOTES

DATE SPROUTED

DATE TRANSPLANTED

LOCATION AND LIGHT

NAME OF SEED

DATE SOWN

NOTES

DATE SPROUTED

DATE TRANSPLANTED

LOCATION AND LIGHT

TAKING CUTTINGS

Softwood cuttings for trees and shrubs are best taken in early spring and potted by mid summer. Take your cuttings from soft, flexible, non-flowering young shoots.

Greenwood cuttings for berry fruits are best taken in late spring or early summer. The base of the stem is firmer than softwood cuttings as it has had longer to mature.

NAME OF SEED

DATE SOWN

DATE SPROUTED

DATE TRANSPLANTED

LOCATION AND LIGHT

NOTES

NAME OF SEED

DATE SOWN

DATE SPROUTED

DATE TRANSPLANTED

LOCATION AND LIGHT

NOTES

NAME OF SEED

DATE SOWN

NOTES

DATE SPROUTED

DATE TRANSPLANTED

LOCATION AND LIGHT

NAME OF SEED

DATE SOWN

NOTES

DATE SPROUTED

DATE TRANSPLANTED

LOCATION AND LIGHT

NAME OF SEED

DATE SOWN

NOTES

DATE SPROUTED

DATE TRANSPLANTED

LOCATION AND LIGHT

NAME OF SEED

DATE SOWN

NOTES

DATE SPROUTED

DATE TRANSPLANTED

LOCATION AND LIGHT

NAME OF SEED

DATE SOWN

NOTES

DATE SPROUTED

DATE TRANSPLANTED

LOCATION AND LIGHT

NAME OF SEED

DATE SOWN

NOTES

DATE SPROUTED

DATE TRANSPLANTED

LOCATION AND LIGHT

NAME OF SEED

DATE SOWN

NOTES

DATE SPROUTED

DATE TRANSPLANTED

LOCATION AND LIGHT

NAME OF SEED

DATE SOWN

NOTES

DATE SPROUTED

DATE TRANSPLANTED

LOCATION AND LIGHT

PHOTOSYNTHESIS

Is the process by which green plants use sunlight to synthesize nutrients from carbon dioxide and water.

Leaves have large surfaces to absorb maximum sunlight. Waxy surfaces conserve water.

Plants are the only living organism that can make their own food.

NAME OF SEED

DATE SOWN

NOTES

DATE SPROUTED

DATE TRANSPLANTED

LOCATION AND LIGHT

NAME OF SEED

DATE SOWN

NOTES

DATE SPROUTED

DATE TRANSPLANTED

LOCATION AND LIGHT

PLANTING LOG

EDIBLES

NAME OF PLANT

VARIETY

ACQUIRED FROM

DATE PLANTED

LOCATION

EXPECTED HARVEST DATE

ACTUAL HARVEST DATE

HARVEST DESCRIPTION

PEST PROBLEMS

NOTES

NAME OF PLANT

VARIETY

ACQUIRED FROM

DATE PLANTED

LOCATION

EXPECTED HARVEST DATE

ACTUAL HARVEST DATE

HARVEST DESCRIPTION

PEST PROBLEMS

NOTES

NAME OF PLANT

VARIETY

ACQUIRED FROM

DATE PLANTED

LOCATION

EXPECTED HARVEST DATE

ACTUAL HARVEST DATE

HARVEST DESCRIPTION

PEST PROBLEMS

NOTES

NAME OF PLANT

VARIETY

ACQUIRED FROM

DATE PLANTED

LOCATION

EXPECTED HARVEST DATE

ACTUAL HARVEST DATE

HARVEST DESCRIPTION

PEST PROBLEMS

NOTES

NAME OF PLANT

VARIETY

ACQUIRED FROM

DATE PLANTED

LOCATION

EXPECTED HARVEST DATE

ACTUAL HARVEST DATE

HARVEST DESCRIPTION

PEST PROBLEMS

NOTES

WEEDS

BINDWEED

THISTLE

DANDELION

Fill empty spaces so there's no room for weeds to grow.

BUTTERCUP

Use vinegar
to eradicate
baby weeds.

NAME OF PLANT

VARIETY

NOTES

ACQUIRED FROM

DATE PLANTED

LOCATION

EXPECTED HARVEST DATE

ACTUAL HARVEST DATE

HARVEST DESCRIPTION

PEST PROBLEMS

NAME OF PLANT

VARIETY

NOTES

ACQUIRED FROM

DATE PLANTED

LOCATION

EXPECTED HARVEST DATE

ACTUAL HARVEST DATE

HARVEST DESCRIPTION

PEST PROBLEMS

NAME OF PLANT

VARIETY

ACQUIRED FROM

DATE PLANTED

LOCATION

EXPECTED HARVEST DATE

ACTUAL HARVEST DATE

HARVEST DESCRIPTION

PEST PROBLEMS

NOTES

NAME OF PLANT

VARIETY

ACQUIRED FROM

DATE PLANTED

LOCATION

EXPECTED HARVEST DATE

ACTUAL HARVEST DATE

HARVEST DESCRIPTION

PEST PROBLEMS

NOTES

NAME OF PLANT

VARIETY

ACQUIRED FROM

DATE PLANTED

LOCATION

EXPECTED HARVEST DATE

ACTUAL HARVEST DATE

HARVEST DESCRIPTION

PEST PROBLEMS

NOTES

NAME OF PLANT

VARIETY

ACQUIRED FROM

DATE PLANTED

LOCATION

EXPECTED HARVEST DATE

ACTUAL HARVEST DATE

HARVEST DESCRIPTION

PEST PROBLEMS

NOTES

ORNAMENTALS

NAME OF PLANT

ACQUIRED FROM

LOCATION

BLOOM COLOUR

BLOOM FRAGRANCE

FOLIAGE QUALITY

EXPECTED HEIGHT

ACTUAL HEIGHT YR 1

ACTUAL HEIGHT YR 2

PEST PROBLEMS

NOTES

NAME OF PLANT

ACQUIRED FROM

NOTES

LOCATION

BLOOM COLOUR

BLOOM FRAGRANCE

FOLIAGE QUALITY

EXPECTED HEIGHT

ACTUAL HEIGHT YR 1

ACTUAL HEIGHT YR 2

PEST PROBLEMS

NAME OF PLANT

ACQUIRED FROM

LOCATION

BLOOM COLOUR

BLOOM FRAGRANCE

FOLIAGE QUALITY

EXPECTED HEIGHT

ACTUAL HEIGHT YR 1

ACTUAL HEIGHT YR 2

PEST PROBLEMS

NOTES

NAME OF PLANT

ACQUIRED FROM

LOCATION

BLOOM COLOUR

BLOOM FRAGRANCE

FOLIAGE QUALITY

EXPECTED HEIGHT

ACTUAL HEIGHT YR 1

ACTUAL HEIGHT YR 2

PEST PROBLEMS

NOTES

NAME OF PLANT

ACQUIRED FROM

NOTES

LOCATION

BLOOM COLOUR

BLOOM FRAGRANCE

FOLIAGE QUALITY

EXPECTED HEIGHT

ACTUAL HEIGHT YR 1

ACTUAL HEIGHT YR 2

PEST PROBLEMS

NAME OF PLANT

ACQUIRED FROM

NOTES

LOCATION

BLOOM COLOUR

BLOOM FRAGRANCE

FOLIAGE QUALITY

EXPECTED HEIGHT

ACTUAL HEIGHT YR 1

ACTUAL HEIGHT YR 2

PEST PROBLEMS

NAME OF PLANT

ACQUIRED FROM

LOCATION

BLOOM COLOUR

BLOOM FRAGRANCE

FOLIAGE QUALITY

EXPECTED HEIGHT

ACTUAL HEIGHT YR 1

ACTUAL HEIGHT YR 2

PEST PROBLEMS

NOTES

ENCOURAGING WILDLIFE TO VISIT

Ponds are a hotbed for wildlife. But if you don't have space or inclination for a pond, just leave a corner of your garden to grow wild. Even just a small patch of long grass will encourage small animals to drop by.

NAME OF PLANT

ACQUIRED FROM

NOTES

LOCATION

BLOOM COLOUR

BLOOM FRAGRANCE

FOLIAGE QUALITY

EXPECTED HEIGHT

ACTUAL HEIGHT YR 1

ACTUAL HEIGHT YR 2

PEST PROBLEMS

NAME OF PLANT

ACQUIRED FROM

LOCATION

BLOOM COLOUR

BLOOM FRAGRANCE

FOLIAGE QUALITY

EXPECTED HEIGHT

ACTUAL HEIGHT YR 1

ACTUAL HEIGHT YR 2

PEST PROBLEMS

NOTES

NAME OF PLANT

ACQUIRED FROM

LOCATION

BLOOM COLOUR

BLOOM FRAGRANCE

FOLIAGE QUALITY

EXPECTED HEIGHT

ACTUAL HEIGHT YR 1

ACTUAL HEIGHT YR 2

PEST PROBLEMS

NOTES

NAME OF PLANT

ACQUIRED FROM

NOTES

LOCATION

BLOOM COLOUR

BLOOM FRAGRANCE

FOLIAGE QUALITY

EXPECTED HEIGHT

ACTUAL HEIGHT YR 1

ACTUAL HEIGHT YR 2

PEST PROBLEMS

NAME OF PLANT

ACQUIRED FROM

LOCATION

BLOOM COLOUR

BLOOM FRAGRANCE

FOLIAGE QUALITY

EXPECTED HEIGHT

ACTUAL HEIGHT YR 1

ACTUAL HEIGHT YR 2

PEST PROBLEMS

NOTES

NAME OF PLANT

ACQUIRED FROM

NOTES

LOCATION

BLOOM COLOUR

BLOOM FRAGRANCE

FOLIAGE QUALITY

EXPECTED HEIGHT

ACTUAL HEIGHT YR 1

ACTUAL HEIGHT YR 2

PEST PROBLEMS

FERTILIZER
APPLICATION
RECORD

DATE

TYPE

DATE

TYPE

DATE

TYPE

DATE

TYPE

LIFECYCLE OF A WORM

Young worm

Worm makes egg cocoons

Worm hatches

Worm reproduces – either
through mating or asexually

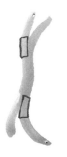

DATE

TYPE

PEST AND
DISEASE
PROBLEMS

DATE	PLANT TYPE	TREATMENT AND NOTES

DATE	PLANT TYPE	TREATMENT AND NOTES

Slugs hate caffeine!

Try using old coffee grounds around the base of your plants to repel them.

DATE	PLANT TYPE	TREATMENT AND NOTES

DATE	PLANT TYPE	TREATMENT AND NOTES

DATE	PLANT TYPE	TREATMENT AND NOTES

DATE	PLANT TYPE	TREATMENT AND NOTES

PESTS

VIBERNUM BEETLE

SNAILS/SLUGS

CHAFER GRUBS

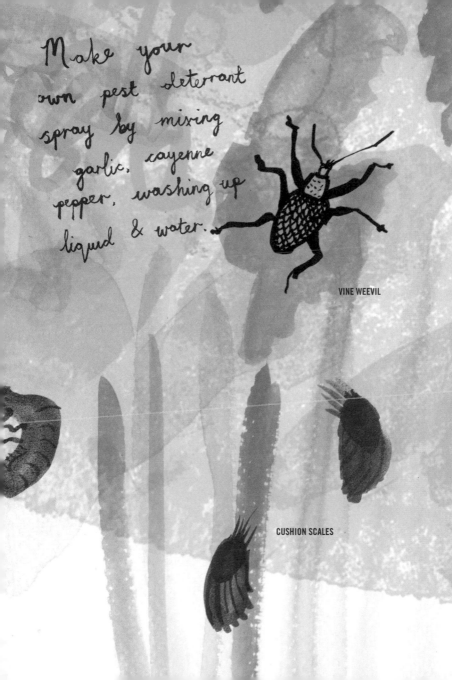

Make your own pest deterrant spray by mixing garlic, cayenne pepper, washing up liquid & water.

VINE WEEVIL

CUSHION SCALES

NOTES

THE YEAR AHEAD

Annual summary for year 20___ :
What worked and what didn't?
What are your plans for next year?

JANUARY

FEBRUARY

MARCH

APRIL

MAY

JUNE

JULY

AUGUST

SEPTEMBER

OCTOBER

NOVEMBER

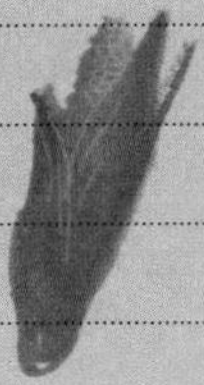

DECEMBER

Published by Cicada Books Limited

Text and illustration by
Rebecca Truscott-Elves
Design by April

British Library Cataloguing-in-
Publication Data.

A CIP record for this book is available
from the British Library.
ISBN: 978-1-908714-13-8

© 2014 Cicada Books Limited

All rights reserved. No part of this
publication may be reproduced stored
in a retrieval system or transmitted in
any form or by any means; electronic,
mechanical, photocopying, recording or
otherwise, without prior permission of
the publisher.

Every effort has been made to trace the
copyright holders, but if any have been
inadvertently overlooked the publishers
will be pleased to make the necessary
arrangements at the first opportunity.

All opinions expressed within this
publication are those of the authors and
not necessarily of the publisher.

Cicada Books Limited
48 Burghley Road
London NW5 1UE

T: +44 207 209 2259
E: ziggy@cicadabooks.co.uk
W: www.cicadabooks.co.uk